T0199033

Sharing Stories of Jesus with Children

Nancy Elizabeth Gainor

Illustrations by Kendall, Clara, Grayson,
Garrett, Hudson, Ford, and Parker Gainor

Copyright © 2020 Nancy Elizabeth Gainor.

All rights reserved. No part of this book may be used or reproduced by any means, graphic, electronic, or mechanical, including photocopying, recording, taping or by any information storage retrieval system without the written permission of the author except in the case of brief quotations embodied in critical articles and reviews.

This book is a work of non-fiction. Unless otherwise noted, the author and the publisher make no explicit guarantees as to the accuracy of the information contained in this book and in some cases, names of people and places have been altered to protect their privacy.

WestBow Press books may be ordered through booksellers or by contacting:

WestBow Press
A Division of Thomas Nelson & Zondervan
1663 Liberty Drive
Bloomington, IN 47403
www.westbowpress.com
1 (866) 928-1240

Because of the dynamic nature of the Internet, any web addresses or links contained in this book may have changed since publication and may no longer be valid. The views expressed in this work are solely those of the author and do not necessarily reflect the views of the publisher, and the publisher hereby disclaims any responsibility for them.

Any people depicted in stock imagery provided by Getty Images are models, and such images are being used for illustrative purposes only.
Certain stock imagery © Getty Images.

Interior Image Credit: Kendall, Clara, Grayson, Garrett, Hudson, Ford, and Parker Gainor

ISBN: 978-1-9736-9333-8 (sc)
ISBN: 978-1-9736-9334-5 (e)

Library of Congress Control Number: 2020910228

Print information available on the last page.

WestBow Press rev. date: 06/15/2020

WESTBOW
PRESS®
A DIVISION OF THOMAS NELSON
& ZONDERVAN

Dedication

The poetic verse is dedicated to my Savior who inspired the words and publication. He is the center of my life and my purpose for living.

Preface

During a time of isolation while safeguarding from the Coronavirus, God placed on my heart a desire to write this book for children. While self-distancing many people contemplated the threat of the deadly virus, leaned upon the Lord and reflected on the meaning of their life. It seemed clear to me that I needed to express a legacy of love for Christ in a creative fashion that appeals to families.

I wanted my family to be able to share the stories of Christ in a simple and yet personalized way that would lead them to a stronger relationship with their Savior. By having the grandchildren illustrate the book, they were able to compile their own interpretation of Jesus and apply the lessons learned. Praise and adoration go out to my illustrators Kendall, Clara, Grayson, Garrett, Hudson, Ford, and Parker Gainor. This could not have been made possible without the help of their parents who under the strain of homeschooling, work and entertaining took time to guide them through the process. Tremendous thanks to Mike, Haley, Brian, Laura, Dan and Mary Gainor. My greatest champion is my husband and best friend John Gainor. His encouragement, faith, creative marketing and love motivated me to achieve this ministry. I am grateful for the validation of friends and family who eagerly await publication and want to share this book with their grandchildren. Joy fills my heart!

All of this would not be possible without my Almighty Lord whose Holy Spirit dwells within me; filing me with a passion for writing and sharing His truth. I am so grateful for His living presence in my life.

Contents

A Message for Mary

Carrying a heavy basin
of water from the well
Mary sees an angel
his message to tell.
Mary has been chosen
a mother to become
baby Jesus she'll deliver
God's precious son.
Courageous is her response
never doubting in her faith
this young virgin only asks
the process it will take.
Engaged to her fiancé,
Joseph must understand
these heavenly matters
are unknown to man.
Mary sings a song of praise
her humble spirit soars
God Almighty truly loves her
who could ask for more?

A Message for Mary
Clara Gainor age 8

Kissing Cousins

Elizabeth is excited
she is going to have a son.
She has waited many years
he'll be her only one.
Today her cousin's coming
she waits keenly by the door.
Mary has arrived
she's traveled very far.
As soon as she sees Mary
her baby, John, will kick.
God's truth is revealed
it emerges from her lips.
Blessed are you Mary
for the child you will bear.
Jesus is our Messiah
for his people he will care.
The cousins hug each other
God's miracles are praised.
His plan for these sweet babies
will change the nation's ways

Donkey Ride

Everyone is traveling
coming near and far
to register in Bethlehem
orders from Caesar.
Taxes are required
people must pay
Mary climbs upon the donkey
Joseph leads the way.
Many days of walking
hunger, thirst and sweat
Joseph always worries
is it Mary's due date yet?
The parents are frightened
faith will see them through
God's plan for the birth of Jesus
is to save me and you.

Donkey Ride
Kendall Gainor age 10

Starry Sky

Sheep are bleating
the shepherd is alone.
The moon is shining
another day is done.
The air is still
the fire glows;
it offers him peace,
it warms his toes.
An angel appears
glory all around
Gabriel's message
is the only sound.
Good news and joy
is declared on this day.
A savior has been born
he lies in the hay
of a stable under a star
beautiful and bright
easy to find
on a very dark night.
What seems like stars
are angels up above.
This special night
is filled with love

Starry Sky
Garrett Gainor age 7

Manger Magic

In Bethlehem a star
radiates above.
Parents hold a baby
filled with love.
Cows are mooing
chickens give a cluck
donkeys are quiet
wrapped cloth is tucked.
This baby's birth
is no ordinary one
for lying in the manger
is God's own son.
Joseph and Mary's journey
has come to an end
when the inn they were seeking
was filled to the brim.
God has provided
the perfect place of birth.
Tiny Jesus isn't crying
precious is his worth.
He has arrived
our Messiah, our friend.

Shining light in a darkened world,
a reign that will not end.
A Savior, Emmanuel
mighty powerful is he
but, for now in this moment
Mary rocks him gently.
He is her little son
cherished in her sight.
The tired parents whisper,
give thanks for this holy night

Manger Magic
Clara Gainor age 8

Bright Star

Three astronomers
study the star
they hope to follow
near and far.
Their destination
is a holy one
nestled in the arms
of his loving mom.
Packing up camels,
food, clothing they take
a journey has begun
many miles they will make.
At last this bright star
rests above the place
where a cherished Jesus
has a smile on his face.
Frankincense and myrrh
and gold they bestow
upon the little Messiah
while bowing low.
Worshiping Jesus
in a humble way
the three wise men
show us how to pray.
Search for Jesus
he lives in your heart.
He is always with you
right from the start.

Bright Star
Kendall Gainor age 10

Pledge

Climbing the steps
leading to church
the little boy Jesus'
feet sway with a lurch.
Proud parents reach out
and steady his hand.
Today is the pledge
given until he's a man.
A trip to the alter
Rabbi's words proclaim.
The family agrees
to honor God's name.
Together they'll worship
apart they will pray
teaching of scripture
will be read every day.
A love of God
will foster joy.
A destiny fulfilled
the Lord is a boy.

Pledge
Ford Gainor age 3

Lost and Found

At twelve the boy Jesus
is off to a feast.
Passover draws crowds
they come to find peace.
Listening to rabbis
sharing in the fun,
food is delicious
children will run.
Joseph and Mary
return to the road
assuming Jesus is
helping others load.
They travel for days
and discover he's gone.
With fear in their hearts
they return to the throng.
Looking everywhere
high and low

they discover him
with teachers in tow.
Angry and frustrated
they question his concern.
"I'm safe in my father's house
when will you learn?"

Hammers and Nails

Nazareth is home
to a boy now a man.
A carpenter by trade
a hammer in his hand.
A father he loved
taught him everything he knew.
Now working alone
some days he feels blue.
Cutting and sanding
precisions just right,
traveling to cities
often at night.
A father and son
whose love forged a bond
lasting stories that
will forever go on.
Caring and creating
a labor of love
now Joseph observes
from heaven above.

Jesus has learned
life lessons from dad
now a new career's beginning
from the one he has had.
God has a plan and
together they'll go
his will to be done
now and tomorrow.

Hammers and Nails
Garrett Gainor age 7

Honey and Locusts

Honey and locusts
a man many fear
shouting redemption
for all to hear.
John the Baptist
with tangled hair
is a sight to see
like a wet bear.
He dips the believers
River Jordan is cold.
They shout "Halleluiah!
I'm saved now behold!"
Along comes a stranger
who is sinless by name.
Christ has arrived
to be baptized the same.
God's approval echoes
thunderous words are said.
Suddenly, a dove appears
water covers Jesus' head.
A divine moment
captured hearts
a humble beginning
an electric start.

Honey and Locusts
Kendall Gainor age 10

Dry Mouth

Critters crawl across
hot, grainy sand.
The thirst is too much
for this holy man.
40 days and 40 nights
in the desert
he's quite a sight.
Satan arrives to save the day.
He offers help
it's on the way.
If only our Messiah
will bow down to him
then all his problems
would seem so slim.
Refusing surrender
Jesus digs in his heels,
relies on his faith no
matter how he feels.
His belief marks a victory
Christ will always win.
Count on the Savior
the one without sin.

Fishing

Boats are idled
a net is cast.
The bait is useless
no fish to be had.
Nothing is biting
heated words are said.
It's getting frustrating
mouths need to be fed.
Along comes friend Jesus
who suggests a repeat.
The fish jam the nets
there is plenty to eat.
He holds conversations
seems to know their heart.
Then asks them to follow
they begin a fresh start.
His words of wisdom
will be shared and then
instead of the fish
the disciples catch men.

Fishing
Grayson Gainor age 8

15

Red, Red Wine

Music is playing,
songs are sung.
The wedding feast
has just begun.
There will be days
to drink and eat
best of everything
at their feet.
A cousin's invitation
Mary and Jesus attend;
but, after several days
flow of wine will end.
Wine so important
for heartfelt toasts
has finally run dry
at the end, needed most.
Encouraged by Mary
he taps vessels of stone.
Soon the clear water
becomes red wine alone.
Servants are amazed
only they understand

first miracle happened
with the touch of his hand.
The finest wine is served
the wedding is a hit
Jesus' glory is revealed
in a basin with a lid.

Red Red Wine
Kendall Gainor age 10

Temple Trashed

Sounds of moaning animals
trapped within a cage.
Merchants holler loudly
foul smells an outrage.
The temple at Passover
changed and furthermore
becomes a marketplace
just a dirty, outside store.
With a whip in hand
Jesus nears the place,
frustration mounting
fury on his face.
Tables are toppled
he shouts, "Get out"
animals scatter
children pout.
He hurdles a statement
many ignore
"Temple destroyed,
three days restored."
It is a prediction
how his life will end
in three days
he will rise again.

Thirsty

Bucket is dropped
deep in the well.
Water is drawn
a story to tell.
Samaritan woman
stranger to most
just met Jesus
unexpected host.
Strange Jewish man
who knows her name
treats her with love
never be the same.
He spoke of the water
living spirit, a sip
she never will thirst
once it touches her lip.
He is our well
of which we can drink.
Thirst for the one
who knows how we think.

Thirsty
Clara Gainor Age 8

Get Well

Simon Peter's mom
is sick in bed.
Can't move a muscle,
fever in her head.
Jesus is visiting,
meals to prepare.
Everything on hold
she really does care.
Jesus takes her hand,
pulls her to her feet.
A miracle occurs
she's able to fix meat.
Singing in the kitchen
the disciples offer praise.
Mother is all better
all hands are raised.
Everyone is fed
there is joy all around.
A personal touch from Christ
is where his love is found

Go Away

Church is packed,
all the pews filled.
Jesus at the podium
everything is still.
Scroll is unrolled,
scripture is read.
"I am the Messiah",
his words are said.
Fists are tightened,
threats are made.
"He has the nerve
to claim he can save."
This is just a boy
from the hood.
No special powers
this is not good.
He claims to be a Savior
sent from God above.
"Let's rid ourselves of Jesus
the one we used to love."
Nazarenes reject
the son of God, our light.
Now he leaves his hometown
to safety he takes flight.

Go Away
Garrett Gainor age 7

20

Skin

Hiding in a colony
far away from town.
"I'm a leper," he announces
everyone will frown.
Skin with blisters,
watery sores,
ashamed and sad
can't take it anymore.
Others will run
but Jesus stays.
Touches the skin
doesn't shy away.
Leper is cleansed,
blemishes removed
a miracle performed
skin like new!
Forever changed,
healed at last
a new beginning
a forgotten past.

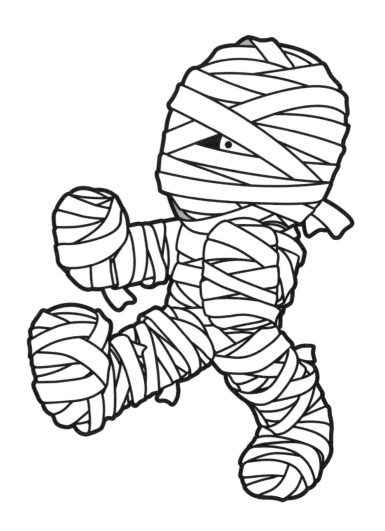

Friends of Faith

Room is crowded
every inch of the floor,
too many people
stuffed in the door.
Jesus is teaching
eyes fixed on him
healing and miracles
he's without sin.
Branches on the roof
opened wide.
Men find a way
to get friend inside.
Slowly he's lowered
on a platform of wood.
Paraplegic needs healing
help if he could.
The faith of the four
impresses our king.
The man gets up,
starts to sing.
Takes his mat
heading home
a miracle occurs
Jesus well known.

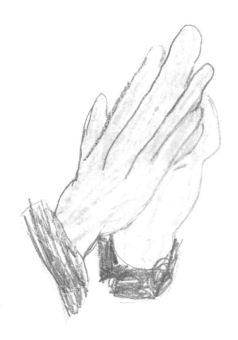

Friends of Faith
Grayson Gainor age 8

Nap time

"Sabbath "says the Pharisees
"is a time of rest."
You shouldn't do anything
this is what's best
Jesus doesn't take a nap
his work is never done.
Healing, caring, sharing too
he is God's only son.
Invalid lies crying
beside a soothing pool.
Jesus heals his body
everything is cool.
A withered hand emerges
behind a tattered cloak.
Jesus touches gently
now it's healed not broke.
Pharisees are angry
Jesus disobeyed.
Now they're out to get him
the framework has been laid.
God the father loves us
seven days a week
go to him in prayer for
he will never sleep.

Clara Gainor age 8

23

Upside down

Thousands are seated
upon the hill.
Jesus is speaking
it is a thrill!
His words are confusing
this isn't the way
we live our life
day by day.
What the world thinks
doesn't matter.
Ideas upside down
a mad hatter.
His words are spoken,
Jesus is wise
it catches the breath
heart beats inside.
Those who are suffering
mournful and meek
will be comforted
receive what they seek.
Those who are hungry
will be fed.

Peacemakers shine
followers led.
The pure in heart
will bear a crown.
Suffering eventually
upside down.
Christ calls us to
examine our life.
Turn it around
and make it right.

Get Up

Wooden casket,
weeping mom
such a sad time
so forlorn.
Funeral procession
winding road
many mourners
it is cold.
Jesus sees her
feels her pain,
words unspoken
won't be the same.
Mom doesn't ask
for help from him.
Her heart is broken
future looks grim.
Her son has passed
the loss is great
he needs to be buried
before it's too late.
"Young man get up,"
Jesus says to the boy.

He opens his eyes
then there is joy.
Alive, alive
a miracle today.
Life after death
in Christ there's a way.

Smelling Sweet

Table is set
food is the best.
Many are present
Jesus prized guest.
Laughing and chatting
the room is a buzz,
a door flies open
there is a hush.
A woman enters
reputation well known.
Questionable behavior
not allowed in this home.
Her eyes meet Jesus
rushes to his side.
Tears fall on his feet
overwhelmed she cries,
Her hair is a towel
his feet are cleaned.
Her humble heart
to the Master is seen.
Expensive perfume
sprinkled and splashed.
Her love for the Lord

will always last.
Simon the Pharisee
aghast at the sight
yells at the woman
she is a fright.
Jesus forgives her
then turns to the host
"Her respect reveals
she loves me the most."

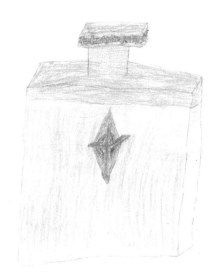

Smelling Sweet
Kendall Gainor age 10

Rocking Boat

Thunder is booming
lightning strikes bright.
Waves are towering
disciples a fright.
Boat is rocking
will this end?
Jesus is sleeping
so calmly again.
Fearing their life
scared to drown
the disciples shake Jesus
to bring him around.
Raising his hands
the storm will end.
'Why don't you trust me?"
he asks them again.
He is our Lord
who created it all.
Forever turn to Jesus
he hears your call.
Peace can be found
Jesus in your heart
be still and listen
you are never apart.

Rocking Boat
Grayson Gainor age 8

Oink Oink

Dark and damp tunnel
is home to a man
frightens so many
no doctors at hand.
Possessed and tormented
it's peace that he seeks.
Christ knows his name
Legion he will meet.
Satan has hurt him
pain fills his life.
He wants to return
to days without strife.
"Come out of this man
spirit so evil."
Jesus is powerful,
protects his people.
Spirits request
to go into the swine.
The pigs start oinking
now is the time.
Herd rushes down
in the river they run.

Pigs cannot swim
spoils demon's fun.
Jesus knows our thoughts,
our words, our deeds.
When we suffer
he meets our needs.

Band-Aid

Bled for 12 years
seems never to end
she knows in Jesus
illness will mend.
Mingling among
swarming crowd,
weaves in and out
noise is so loud.
His touch of power
spreads from his robe
will cure her ailment
and then he spoke.
"Who touched my clothes,
pulled at the hem?"
she trembled and cried
"It's me not them."
Healing power exits
woman is cured,
suffering subsides
faith is pure.

Trusting in the Lord
best thing we can do.
He truly knows our heart
he cares for me and you.

Hudson Gainor age 4

Light

Jesus is relaxing
in a house so still,
tired from teaching
listens to God's will.
The door bursts open
two men stumble in.
Neither can see
blind not from sin.
"Heal us," they beg
as they bow on the floor.
In faith you will be
not blind anymore.
He crafts a mud ball
rests it on the eyes
Light filters in
what a surprise!
Colors so vibrant,
family and friends
they see everything
joy never ends.

Shouting and praising
grateful so much
finally healed
with only a touch.
Steadfast faith
Jesus is Lord!
He is our true light
for evermore.

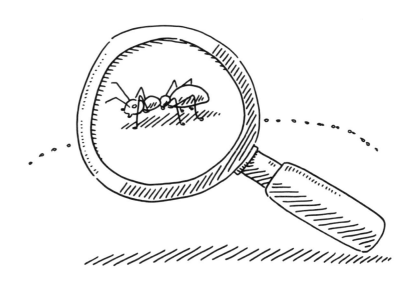

Ready, Set, Go

Jesus is preparing
for this special day.
The disciples are leaving
they are on their way.
Teaching them scripture
God's truth to share,
powers now been given
miracles to bear.
Sword of scripture,
faith a shield
minister to others
God's truth to yield.
Two by two
work to be done,
harvest the field
for God's own son.
Jesus knows the danger
wolf dressed as sheep.
It's time they move on
in prayers will he keep.
A light unto their path,
mission without end
Jesus is their Savior
but also their friend.

Ready, Set, Go
Parker Gainor age 2

Bottomless Basket

Sunrays bake
the hillside warm.
A little boy
sits next to mom.
Thousands are here
traveled so far
want to hear Jesus
he's a superstar.
Everyone is hungry
no food to eat,
tired and weary
callused feet.
No local places
where they can go
get something to eat
it is needed so.
Five barley loaves
in a basket small,
also two fish
will it help at all?
He grabs the basket
skips to the Lord.

A prayer is said
5,000 or more
fed and full
a miracle complete.
Now there's even
leftovers to eat.

Bottomless Basket
Hudson Gainor age 4

Ghost

Wind is whistling
moon is full,
boat is swaying
strong current pull.
Disciples are scared
it's late at night
what seems a ghost
gives them a fright.
The shadow walks
across the lake.
Could it be Jesus?
They begin to shake.
His voice assuring
keeps them calm.
Peter leaps over
says he is wrong,
depends on himself
doesn't lean on Christ.
Takes Jesus' hand
then looks down twice.
Beginning to sink
he panics, "I'll drown!"

The Lord lifts him up
won't let him down.
Fix your eyes
on Christ above
count on him
he's full of love.

Parker Gainor age 2

Silent

Not one little sound
or even pin drop.
All is silent
ears won't pop.
Deaf his whole life
not hearing a word,
missing conversations
a singing bird.
Tongue doesn't work
a hardship for sure
is this the prophet
who can find a cure?
His friends seek Jesus
asking for help
man is desperate
can't even yelp.
Privately Christ places
fingers in ears,
spits onto tongue
then he hears.
Speaking, hearing plainly
overwhelmed with jubilee

now the deaf-mute man
is just like you and me.
Praise our Savior often
many blessings he gives
eyes, ears, heart open
that's the way to live.

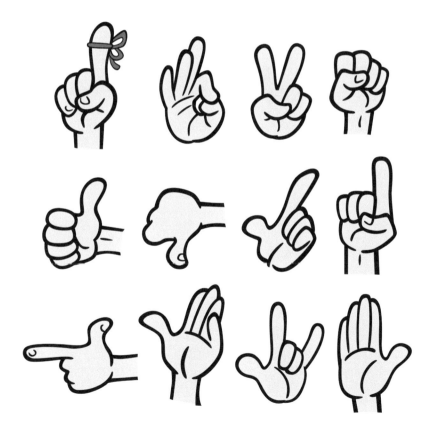

Surprise

Climbing up the mountain
Peter, James and John
wonder where they're going
Jesus comes along.
At the very top
a change is taking place
now there is brightness
dazzling Jesus' face.
Clothes not the same
glowing, vivid white
seems as if his body
is now made of light.
Moses and Elijah
appear by his side.
Jesus will leave soon
it makes disciples cry.
Peter has a thought
three shelters he'll erect,
a cloud soon develops
God's voice he won't forget.

"Jesus is my chosen son
listen to him", said he.
"Shelters aren't required
you're together eternally."

Grayson Gainor Age 8

Seed

Seizures unending
rolled eyes, flapping arms,
demon-possessed child
parents alarmed.
It is getting dangerous
in fire he is burned.
Dad pleads with Jesus
no place to turn.
Crowd is watching
no one believes.
Demon is cast out
everyone relieved.
Why had disciples failed
to do the job alone?
"Doubt stood in their way"
he said with scolding tone.
"When you have faith
like a mustard seed
mountains can move
if only you believe."

Clara Gainor age 8

36

Childlike faith

Walking on a dusty road
to Capernaum disciples go.
Arguing as to who is best
Jesus tells them "No!"
A lesson in the making
a little child is called
there is no room for egos
in the kingdom of God.
When this child is welcomed
in my name you see
God is also welcomed
for my father sent me.
Least among you is great
think like a child,
joyful and kind
no pride allowed.
Children show us love,
affection and obey.
This spiritual character
is the Christian way.

Kendall Gainor age 10

Host

Cooking and cleaning
Martha's tired and sore.
Mary sits waiting
Jesus at the door.
Preparations perfect
Martha's goal.
Mary only wants
what's best for the soul.
Grumbling, Martha tells him,
"This isn't fair!"
She is run ragged
Mary doesn't care.
Jesus says, "It's vital
God's truth to hear.
It's time to rest awhile
sit down, have cheer."
We are very busy
lists long in length
Jesus top priority
he is our strength.

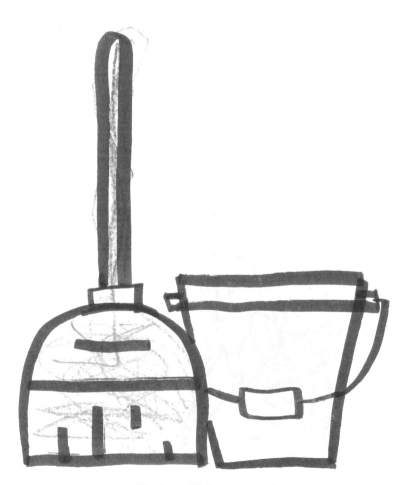

Parker Gainor age 2

Cry

Lazarus has died
he was Jesus' friend.
Brother of Martha and Mary
faithful to the end.
Upon Jesus' arrival
the girls question him,
"Why didn't you save him?"
his many tears begin.
Tomb is opened
smell is too much.
Observers retreat
a quiet hush.
In a loud voice
his name Jesus calls.
They hold their breath
stumbling he falls.
"He's alive!" crowd cheers.
"How can this be?
Lazarus resurrected
the proof we can see."
Many people witnessed
God's power this day
becoming a Christian
Jesus is the way.

Grayson Gainor age 8

Treetop

Tiny man sits up
in a stately tree
for the Savior Jesus
one he wants to see.
Perfect view above
people jammed below
watching birds and clouds
a gentle breeze flows.
Tax collector his trade
disliked by many
he takes their wages
keeps every penny.
Jesus soon appears
beneath the sycamore tree
offers dinner plans
together there is glee.
Scrambling down the branch
surprised at the request
Zacchaeus makes a vow
he'll pay back all the rest.
Today salvation comes
to a wee little man
who gave his heart to Christ
for him he takes a stand.

Treetop
Grayson Gainor age 8

Hosanna

Cheering in the distance
praises to be heard.
Jesus rides a donkey
he doesn't say a word.
Upon the path before him
coats and palm fronds lay.
"Messiah!" they proclaim.
"Our help is on the way."
King of Kings they call him
the one they've waited for
truly Jesus understands
he's so much that and more.
Although the crowd is merry
his thoughts sadden him.
He knows the end is coming
God's will always wins.
Shout loud hosannas
bow down before the king
his love for you abundant
in gratitude now sing.

Kendall Gainor age 10

Let's Eat

Feast of the Passover
last gathering of friends.
Together in the upper room
he knows it soon will end.
Judas a betrayer
has money on his mind.
Jesus says, "Get going
now is the time."
Bread is for his body
red wine is his blood
last supper complete
Christ' work on earth done.
Long will we remember
as communion we partake
the sacrifice Christ made
because of sins we make.

Ford Gainor age 3

Arrest

After the last supper
a garden to pray.
Gethsemane so quiet
tonight is where he'll stay.
Disciples standing guard
soon asleep will fall.
Alone our Lord is praying
envisioning it all.
The torture and the pain
his death will surly come.
"Please remove this cup"
to the father says the son.
Perspiration turns to blood
dripping down his cheek.
Anguished he obeys
God's will is what he seeks.
Soldiers feet tread on the path
Judas leads the pack
kisses Jesus' cheek
there is no turning back.

Arrested he is hauled away
disciples flee and hide.
Tossed in prison all alone
no one by his side.

Hudson Gainor age 4

Cross

Carrying a heavy cross
the Lord climbs up the hill.
Calvary it is called
the punishment to fill.
Jesus has been tried
guilty on all counts.
No crime he's committed
Pharisees want him out.
A crown of thorns he wears
beaten and called names.
Nails in hands and feet
on a cross he hangs in shame.
Offering to save
the sinner next to him.
Christ always thinks of others
forgives them of their sin.
"Why have you forsaken me?"
he cries out in pain.
God turns his head in sorrow
access to heaven we gain.
Finished, the last breath he takes
earthquakes begin to roar.
Dead bodies rise, lightning strikes

shakes God's anger to the core.
Separated from our God
Holy of Holies torn open.
Now we come unto the Lord
what's in our hearts is spoken.
Jesus is our Savior
he died for you and me.
His sacrifice for our sins
brings life eternally.

Cross
Hudson Gainor Age 4

Alive

Jesus' body is placed
in a tomb cold and dark.
Disciples flee and weep
sorrowful is their heart.
Mary Magdalene comes
to the tomb third day.
Can't believe her eyes
the stone has rolled away.
Enters and sees nothing
cries and leaves the site.
Outside stranger speaks
she turns away in fright.
Knows her name and pain
a gardener she thinks is he.
"They've taken away my Lord.
I am in such misery."
He says, "Beloved Mary
there's a mission to fulfill.
Do not cling to me
It's against God's will.
Seek out the others
spread the good news.

I'm alive, going to heaven
but always with you."
Mary flees the garden
her Lord is alive!
He is resurrected
they will survive.
Jesus sent the Holy Spirit
to dwell within your soul.
Light the world his cherished one
he's alive, let people know.

Kendall Gainor age 10

Your picture of Jesus

What do you love most about Jesus?

Printed in the United States
By Bookmasters